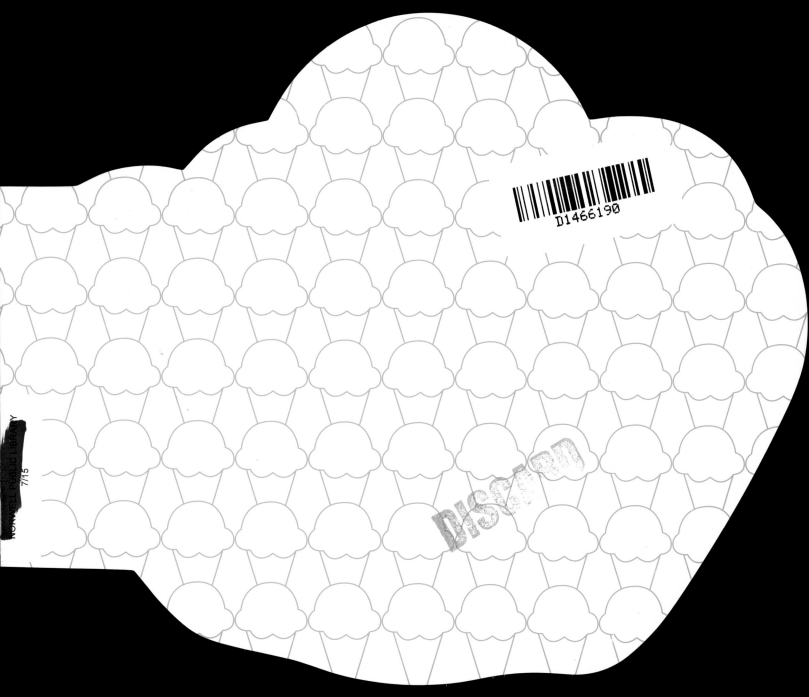

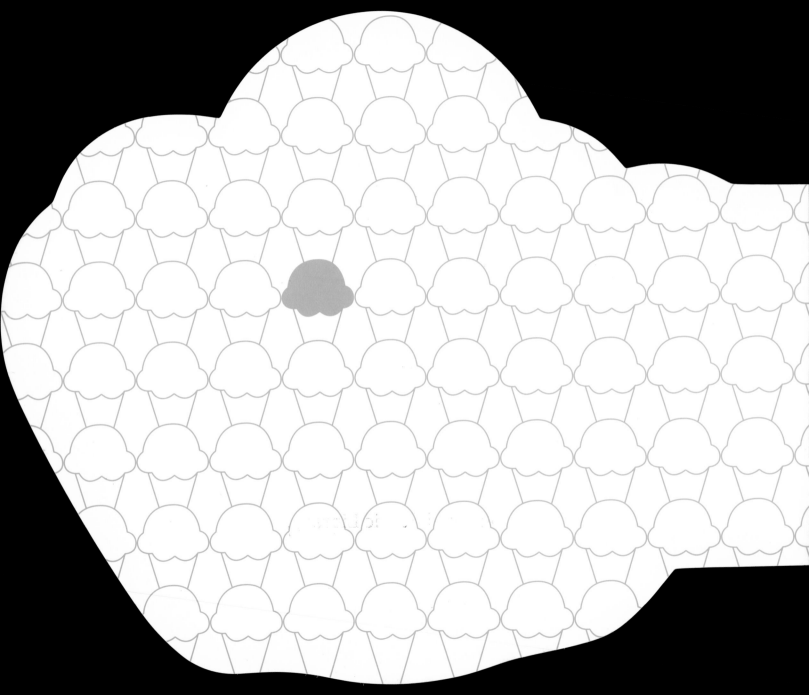

ICE CREAM

50 Easy Recipes

ACADEMIA
BARILLA

EDITED BY
ACADEMIA BARILLA

PHOTOGRAPHY BY
ALBERTO ROSSI
CHEF MARIO GRAZIA

RECIPES BY
CHEF MARIO GRAZIA

TEXT BY
MARIAGRAZIA VILLA

GRAPHIC DESIGN
MARINELLA DEBERNARDI

EDITORIAL COORDINATION ACADEMIA BARILLA
CHATO MORANDI
ILARIA ROSSI
LEANNE KOSINSKI

3

CONTENTS

5

SHIVERS
OF SWEET PLEASURE

Italy, the cradle of the arts in general, can be defined as the cradle of the art of ice cream.
Georges Auguste Escoffier, *Le Guide Culinaire*, 1903

Delicious. Sweet. Always different. Soft, carefree, and at times impertinent. Refreshing and pleasant. In the summer as well as the winter. Often linked with friends, vacations, freedom. If there is one thing that recalls childhood to our taste buds, it is definitely ice cream. Is there anything more playful or exhilarating? What can compare to diving into the embrace of *fior-dilatte*, into the crunchy music of hazelnuts immersed in chocolate, into the infinite tenderness of cream? What can compare to letting yourself be wrapped by the fragrant spiral of mango or passion fruit? Or letting yourself be surprised by the most successful flavor pairings and the most imaginative contrasts in textures, colors and aromas? Ice cream is a true experience. Not just a pleasure for the palate, but a multisensory symphony that caresses the heart and the soul.

A Story that is Long ... and Refreshing
Was Abraham the first man fortunate enough to taste ice cream? According to the Bible, his son Isaac offered him a drink of goat milk and snow, saying "Eat and drink: the sun is torrid and you can cool down." What is certain is that among some ancient peoples, such as the Babylonians, the Egyptians, the Greeks and the Romans, there was a custom of chilling sweet substances, such as juices obtained by squeezing fruit. A recipe recorded by Pliny the Elder tells of how to prepare a sort of sorbet by mixing crushed ice, honey and fruit juice.
A decisive role was played by the Arabs. So much so, that the word "sorbet" may have derived from one of the following two Arab etymons: *sherbet* (sweet snow) or *sharber* (to sip). When

they landed in Sicily in 1827, the Muslims began combining snow from Mount Etna, and the Hyblaean and Madonie Mountains with fruit juices, particularly those of citrus fruit, aromatic herbs, spices and the highly prized cane sugar, to produce delicious and aromatic iced desserts. Nevertheless, ice cream as we know it today is an all-Italian invention.

The Chicken Farmer of Sorbets

"With your permission, I return to my chickens, hoping people will finally leave me alone, and having forgotten me, be satisfied just to enjoy my ice-cream." These were the final words in a letter written by Ruggeri to Caterina de' Medici. We are in the 16th century, and this man, whose first name we do not know, is in all probability the one responsible for bringing sorbet back into fashion by salvaging ancient recipes fallen into disuse during the Medieval Period. Some years before, Ruggeri, a humble chicken farmer, won a culinary competition entitled "The most singular dish ever seen" held at the Medici Court with his "frozen sweet". His recipe for "ice made with sweet and flavored water" was such a success that Caterina de' Medici, betrothed to Henry II, the future king of France, decided to add Ruggeri to her trusted squad of cooks and pastry chefs before departing for Marseille for her wedding celebration. The wedding banquet, held in 1533, was a success, in part due to the formidable sorbets prepared by this Mister Nobody. All of Europe's nobles began to offer Caterina vast amounts of money just to secure him. She refused. However, beyond the Alps, poor Ruggeri was envied and treated with hostility by other cooks, who even resorted to hitting and robbing him. At this point, Ruggeri decided to take off his apron and return to his previous life. It's best to fly back to your nest if you don't want to get your feathers plucked.

The Ice Cream Architect

The second Florentine father of ice cream, Bernardo Buontalenti, also had a weakness for cooking. He was the perfect Renaissance man: architect, painter, sculptor, miniaturist, military engineer and stage designer. It seems that he was also the first to use milk, cream and eggs to make an iced dessert; in this way, conceiving ice cream as we know it today.

In 1559, in honor of the arrival of the Spanish diplomatic mission to Florence, Grand Duke Cosimo I charged Buontalenti with organizing feasts so lavish, as to "leave the foreigners and the Spaniards speechless." The biggest impression on the guests' palates was made by Buontalenti's zabaione and fruit-based ice creams. They were so good that since then, ice cream came to mean something richer and more well-rounded than the classic sorbets, becoming a dessert that was not only refreshing but also nutritional and even more delicious.

The Fisherman of Delights

It was yet another Italian, this time from Catania, to transform ice cream making into a business: not just a delicacy served in the dining halls of nobles, but one sold to the public. Francesco Procopio Cutò "de' Coltelli" (his name was later frenchified to Couteaux), a simple fisherman from Aci Trezza, left for Paris in search of fortune carrying with him a machine for making sorbet. A machine which was tuned by his grandfather Francesco, a clever fisherman who in his free time developed a method for rendering the mixture of fruit, ice and honey more homogeneous. In 1686, after having perfected the machine, Procopio opened the world's first café-ice cream shop in the French capital. Café Procope soon became the preferred gathering spot of Parisian intelligentsia, in part due to its excellent ice creams, praised by the Sun King himself.

In the centuries that followed, the café became a destination for personalities such as Voltaire, Balzac and Hugo. A famous testimony by a friend of Oscar Wilde, recalls the Irish poet and writer's habit of going to Café Procope to reflect about life in front of a nice cup of ice cream.

Cones and Other "Strolling" Varieties

Thanks to Italian ice cream makers, the fame of this cold delicacy propagated across the world arriving as far as the United States, where in 1770, in New York, the Genoa-born Giovanni Bosio opened the first American ice cream shop. In 1903, Vittorio Marchionni, another Italian-American from Cadore, patented the first waffle cone: a true revolution, because up until then it was not customary to eat ice cream while strolling down a street. A precursor of the ice cream cone, the *parigine*, ice cream sandwiched between two wafers, on the other hand, was invented by Giovanni Torre from Sanremo during his stay in Paris at the beginning of the 20th century. The ice cream sandwich also saw the light of day in the French capital. It was conceived a century earlier, in 1803, by another emigrated Italian ice cream maker, the Neapolitan Alessandro Tortoni of Café Napolitaine, a famous locale that often played host to Gioacchino Rossini.

Not Just a Dessert

Based on their ingredients, ice creams can be divided into two groups (in 1830, Vincenzo Agnoletti, a master distiller and nutritional advisor to Marie Louise of Austria, was the first to classify the different types of ice cream): cream-based, if they contain milk, cream, sugar, eggs and other ingredients such as chocolate, coffee, almonds, hazelnuts etc.; and fruit-based, if instead, they contain water (in some cases substituted with milk for a more filling

and creamy product), fruit juice and/or pulp, and sugar. The word sorbet, on the other hand, refers to ice cream that contains no fats, milk or milk derivatives.

Cream-based ice cream is not just delicious, but also nutritionally balanced, because it supplies the correct proportion of proteins, lipids and carbohydrates, in addition to minerals and vitamins. Since milk is one of its main ingredients, it is also relatively rich in calcium, phosphate, vitamin A and B-group vitamins (particularly B1 and B2). It is these nutritional properties that make cream-based ice cream not just a dessert but food, which can substitute, particularly in the summer months, a lunch or a dinner.

Favorites in Italy and Beyond

Academia Barilla, an international center dedicated to the diffusion of Italian cuisine, has selected fifty recipes of this delicious dessert. From ice creams to sorbets, Italian ices and popsicles. From the simpler creations, such as lemon ice cream, to more complicated specialties, such as the Three-Colored Bomb Cake and the Praline Ice Cream Cones. From traditional recipes, such as the timeless chocolate ice cream, to those more original, such as the Mojito popsicle and Moscato d'Asti sorbet.

The chosen recipes include not just Italian-born desserts, such as the Ice Cream Cassata, a frozen version of a typical Sicilian dessert, but also recipes from abroad. Recipes that share the high quality raw ingredients, successful choice of pairings and the festive spirit of the Italian recipes. One example of such a recipe is the Peach Melba, created in 1892 by the French chef, Georges Auguste Escoffier, in honor of the legendary Australian opera singer Helen Porter Mitchell, known by her stage name Nellie Melba, who loved peaches, raspberries and vanilla ice cream.

WHEN ICE CREAM IS MADE AT HOME

Home-made ice cream! Even when compared with the best product of the best artisan ice cream shop, the flavor of an ice cream made with your own hands using natural ingredients is priceless. To prepare a good frozen dessert – that's rich but soft; not quick to melt, but still creamy; energizing but light; refreshing but not cold – you need three things: high quality, fresh ingredients, as fundamental as for any other culinary preparation; the right balance between these ingredients, such that the moist component of the mixture, the only component to freeze, is properly balanced by the water-free and hence non-freezable ingredients (which should constitute 35-40% of the total); and the mandatory, careful compliance with hygienic standards, because everything that is used (both the ingredients and the utensils) is subject to contamination by pathogenic organisms.

When the Cold Becomes Dessert

Making ice cream at home is very easy. The steps can be essentially summarized as follows: dosing and prepping the ingredients (for example, if fresh fruit is used, it must first be washed, cleaned and sliced), amalgamation (which may be done cold or hot, depending on the type of ice cream, but always until a perfectly homogeneous mixture is obtained), setting of the mixture in the refrigerator and churning (which may be done using an ice cream making machine or manually). Next, if the ice cream is not served immediately, it must be frozen in the freezer at a temperature between 7°F (-14°C) and 3°F (-16°C).
Ice cream that is not consumed immediately can be stored in the freezer in closed containers, but it must be remembered that the longer it stays in the freezer, the harder it will become.

The Tools of the Trade

Theoretically, it should be possible to produce your own frozen dessert without the use of an ice cream maker; however, in practice, ice cream as we know it today cannot be made without the help of this fundamental machine. During manual churning, slow freezing of the mixture provokes the formation of larger ice crystals, resulting in a gritty, irregular texture considered a defect in the final product (while being desired in Italian ices).

The home ice cream maker is a scaled down version of an industrial ice cream maker. It works by chilling a mixture of ingredients to a temperature below freezing while stirring continuously to incorporate air into the mixture and augment its volume, obtaining a composite that is soft and creamy, as opposed to a single block of ice. Depending on the coolant used, an ice cream maker may have a built-in freezing mechanism or require pre-chilling of the bowl. The churning time is variable because it depends on the composition of the mixture, air temperature, and cooling power of the machine being used.

Typically, an ice cream is ready when the paddle can no longer shift it, starts to shift it in sections, or is simply no longer able to compress it very much.

In addition to the ice cream maker, the must-have tools are a measuring cup and spoons for measuring out the ingredients; a coarse-mesh and a fine-mesh strainer for eliminating the fibrous portions and impurities from fruit; a scraper spatula, which is essential in ice cream making for preventing waste; an ice cream scooper, which exist in various shapes, sizes and materials; a digital scale for weighing larger ingredients; a

digital probe thermometer for accurately measuring the temperature of both hot and cold ingredients; and an immersion blender for reducing semisolid ingredients such as fruit to the consistency of a puree.

From time to time, you will also need a series of tools that you likely already have in your kitchen cupboard, such as an electric hand mixer to whip cream and egg whites, a juice squeezer, saucepans, spoons, forks, knives, basins, bowls, molds etc.

Suggestions to Follow

Here are some simple tricks for making an excellent ice cream. A common error is to use too much sugar, which not only results in a product that is too sweet, but one that has difficulty freezing. Since sugar serves to maintain ice cream's creamy consistency, if the ice cream maker is not very powerful, too much of this ingredient will prevent the mixture from freezing correctly. Next, the fruit. Every piece must be carefully pureed. Since it is an ingredient with a high water content, any pieces of fruit contained in the ice cream will freeze as soon as it is placed in the freezer. The not so pleasant result will be that of ice crystals crunching between your teeth...

When you pour mixture into the steel bowl of the ice cream maker, where the paddle will transform it into ice cream, you must not exceed the maximum fill line because during churning, the ice cream will augment in volume (by about 25%). When preparing a new ice cream flavor, you should carefully wash both the bowl and the paddle because contamination with a different flavor does not always result pleasant.

Since homemade ice cream loses consistency rather rapidly, never make quantities

that are too large and only store it in the freezer for short periods. Ideally, it should be eaten right out of the ice cream maker.

Some Ice Cream Etiquette

You can serve the ice cream in serving bowls or small cups made of glass, metal or ceramic. The bowls should have a stem and be served on a similar saucer lined with a small napkin. Since homemade ice cream tends to melt quickly (even though the addition of stabilizer and dextrose make it more compact and consistent), it is best to pre-chill the serving bowls for a short period in the refrigerator or freezer, and to fill them right before serving.

Use an ice cream scooper to arrange the ice cream in the serving bowls, forming many small, well-ordered balls. Once positioned, the ice cream can be garnished with whipped cream, fresh and dried fruit, nuts, cookies, waffles, cherries in syrup, sugar flowers... Use shovel-shaped ice cream spoons with a straight tip that enables one to divide the ice cream into portions to be placed in the mouth.

Rectangular ice cream cakes and ice cream bombs or domes should be served precut into slices or wedges, as dictated by their shape, on serving plates lined with a paper doily.

Ice cream, if served at the end of a lunch or a dinner, should be served after coffee. Sorbet, on the other hand, if served during a meal, must be brought to the table between the fish and the meat courses, and have a bold, sour taste serving to cleanse the palate and prepare the stomach for more structured food and wine. It should consist of a small ball of a single flavor served in a small bowl or cup.

PARADISE

Formerly known as "milk snow", sweetened whipped cream, a sweet-tooth's true Eden, has been known in Italy since the 16th century and has been mentioned in the cookbooks of many famous chefs, such as Cristoforo di Messisbugo, who cooked at the Este Court in Ferrara, and Bartolomeo Scappi, who worked in the kitchens of the Vatican under Popes Pius IV and Pius V.

How to Make It

Often used to garnish ice cream with its feather-soft, baroque whirls, sweetened whipped cream is very easy to make. The ingredients for 4-6 people are 1 cup (250 ml) of whipping cream (35% fat) and 2 1/2-3 1/2 tablespoons (30-45 g) of sugar. To prepare it (you will need 5 to 10 minutes), mix the cream (stored at a temperature of 36 to 41°F [2 to 5°C], or it will not whip) with the sugar (the quantity varies with the degree of sweetness desired) in a very large, concave bowl (as it is whipped, cream incorporates air and almost doubles in volume). Then, whip using a whisk or an electric hand mixer until it takes on the classic whipped cream consistency. Store in the refrigerator.

A few tips. For a better result, especially in hot weather, chill the bowl and the whisk or electrical hand mixer attachments in the freezer for a few minutes before use. Don't' exaggerate when whipping the cream or you risk turning it into butter. Whipped cream that becomes runny can be safely whipped again in the same manner as fresh cream. Since cream, both whipped and liquid, has a tendency to absorb odors, it should be stored in the refrigerator in a closed container.

16

ICE CREAM

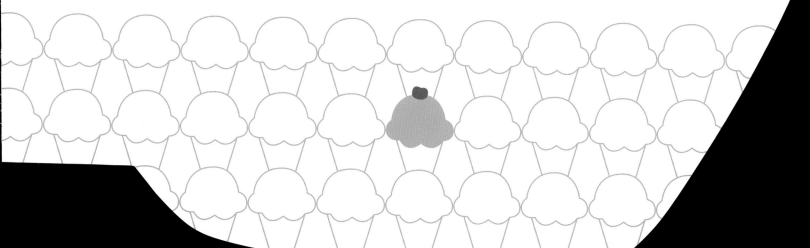

BACIO
ICE CREAM

INGREDIENTS FOR ABOUT 4 CUPS (800 GRAMS) OF ICE CREAM

For the ice cream
1 3/4 cups (375 g) dark chocolate ice cream (recipe page 30)
1 3/4 cups (375 g) custard ice cream (recipe page 48)
1/3 cup (75 g) Piedmont hazelnut paste

For the decoration
chopped Piedmont hazelnuts

METHOD
Using an immersion blender, carefully combine the chocolate
and custard ice creams with the hazelnut paste.
Churn the mixture in an ice cream maker until it is airy and dry in appearance,
i.e. not shiny (the time required depends on the ice cream maker used).
Transfer the Bacio ice cream into individual cups or cones
and sprinkle with chopped hazelnuts.

Preparation time: 1 h - Resting time: 6 h
Difficulty: medium

SHORTBREAD COOKIE ICE CREAM

INGREDIENTS FOR ABOUT 4 CUPS (850 GRAMS) OF ICE CREAM

2 cups (500 ml) whole milk
2/3 cup (120 g) sugar
1/3 cup (80 ml) cream
2 1/2 tbsp. (20 g) powdered skim milk
1 1/3 tbsp. (15 g) dextrose
1 1/2 tsp. (3.5 g) stabilizer for ice cream
4 1/4 oz. (120 g) shortbread cookies

METHOD

In a small saucepan, heat the milk to a temperature of 115°F (45°C). Combine the sugar,
the powdered milk, the dextrose and the stabilizer, and slowly pour into the milk. Bring to 150°F
(65°C). Add the cream and pasteurize at 185°F (85°C). Coarsely chop the shortbread cookies
and add them to the boiling mixture. Quickly cool to 40°F (4°C) by putting the mixture
into a container immersed in a basin with water and ice. Allow to set at 40°F (4°C) for 6 hours.
Blend using an immersion blender before churning the mixture in an ice cream maker
until it is airy and dry in appearance, i.e. not shiny
(the time required depends on the ice cream maker used).
Transfer the ice cream into individual cups or cones and serve.

Preparation time: 1 h - Resting time: 6 h
Difficulty: medium

CHEESECAKE ICE CREAM

INGREDIENTS FOR ABOUT 4 1/2 CUPS (1 KG) OF ICE CREAM

For the ice cream
2 1/2 cups (575 ml) whole milk
1 cup (190 g) sugar
3 tbsp. (23 g) powdered skim milk
2 tsp. (4.5 g) stabilizer
for ice cream

1 tbsp. (13 g) dextrose
1 cup (180 g) spreadable
cheese

For the strawberry sauce
1 3/4 cup (250 g) strawberries

1/2 cup (100 g) sugar
1 1/2 tbsp. (15 g) cornstarch
juice of 1/4 lemon

For the decoration
all butter shortbread cookies

METHOD

In a small saucepan, heat the milk to a temperature of 115°F (45°C). Combine the sugar,
the powdered milk, the dextrose and the stabilizer, and slowly pour into the milk. Bring to 150°F
(65°C) and then pasteurize at 185°F (85°C). Quickly cool to 40°F (4°C) by putting the mixture
into a container immersed in a basin with water and ice. Allow to set at 40°F (4°C) for 6 hours.
Add the cheese and blend using an immersion blender before churning the mixture in an ice
cream maker until it is airy and dry in appearance, i.e. not shiny
(the time required depends on the ice cream maker used).
For the strawberry sauce, blend the strawberries with a mixture of sugar
and cornstarch using an immersion blender. Add the lemon juice and allow to boil
for a few minutes. Cool. Serve the ice cream with the strawberry sauce and top,
if desired, with crumbled shortbread cookies.

Preparation time: 1 h - Resting time: 6 h
Difficulty: medium

WHITE CHOCOLATE ICE CREAM

INGREDIENTS FOR ABOUT 4 1/2 CUPS (1 KG) OF ICE CREAM

1 1/2 cups (350 ml) whole milk
12 1/3 oz. (350 g) white chocolate
1 1/3 cups (300 ml) fiordilatte ice cream mixture (recipe p. 62)

METHOD

Chop the white chocolate and transfer to a bowl.
Add the milk to a small saucepan and bring to a boil.
Pour the milk over the chocolate and blend carefully.
Add fiordilatte ice cream mixture, mix and quickly cool to 40°F (4°C)
by putting the mixture into a container immersed in a basin with water and ice.
Allow to set at 40°F (4°C) for 6 hours.
Freeze by churning in an ice cream maker until the mixture is airy and dry in appearance,
i.e. not shiny (the time required depends on the ice cream maker used).
Transfer the chocolate ice cream into serving cups or cones, and serve.

Preparation time: 1 h - Resting time: 6 h
Difficulty: medium

WHITE CHOCOLATE AND PASSION FRUIT ICE CREAM

INGREDIENTS FOR ABOUT 4 1/2 CUPS (1 KG) OF ICE CREAM

1 cup (200 ml) whole milk
1 cup (235 ml) water
2/3 cup (125 g) sugar
4 1/2 tbsp. (50 g) glucose
1 1/2 tsp. (3.5 g) stabilizer for ice cream
1 1/4 cups (225 g) passion fruit pulp
5 oz. (140 g) white chocolate

METHOD

Chop the white chocolate and transfer to a bowl.
In a small saucepan, heat milk and water to a temperature of 115°F (45°C). Combine the sugar
and the stabilizer. Slowly pour into the milk and then add the glucose. Pasteurize at 185°F (85°C)
and pour over the white chocolate, mixing until the chocolate is completely melted.
Add the passion fruit pulp and quickly cool to 40°F (4°C) by putting the mixture
into a container immersed in a basin with water and ice.
Allow to set at 40°F (4°C) for 6 hours and then freeze by churning in an ice cream maker
until the mixture is airy and dry in appearance, i.e. not shiny (the time required
depends on the ice cream maker used). Transfer the white chocolate
and passion fruit ice creams into individual cups or cones.

Preparation time: 1 h - Resting time: 6 h
Difficulty: medium

ICE CREAM

INGREDIENTS FOR ABOUT 4 1/2 CUPS (1 KG) OF ICE CREAM

1 2/3 cups (400 ml) whole milk
7 tbsp. (50 g) powdered skim milk
1/2 cup (110 g) sugar
3 1/2 tbsp. (40 g) glucose

1 1/2 tsp. (3.5 g) stabilizer for ice cream
1/2 cup (100 ml) cream
1 1/2 cups (200 g) raspberries
3 1/2 oz. (100 g) dark chocolate

METHOD

Chop the chocolate and transfer to a bowl.
In a small saucepan, heat the milk to 115°F (45°C). Combine the sugar, the powdered milk and the stabilizer. Slowly pour into the milk and then add the glucose.
Bring to 150°F (65°C) and add the cream. Pasteurize at 185°F (85°C) and pour over the chocolate, mixing until the chocolate is completely melted. Quickly cool to 40°F (4°C) by putting the mixture into a container immersed in a basin with water and ice.
Allow to set at 40°F (4°C) for 6 hours. Add the raspberries, carefully blend everything using an immersion blender and then freeze by churning in an ice cream maker until the mixture is airy and dry in appearance, i.e. not shiny (the time required depends on the ice cream maker used).
Transfer the chocolate and raspberry ice cream into individual cups or cones.

Preparation time: 1 h - Resting time: 6 h
Difficulty: medium

DARK CHOCOLATE ICE CREAM

INGREDIENTS FOR 3 GENEROUS CUPS (700 GRAMS) OF ICE CREAM

2 cups (500 ml) whole milk
2/3 cup (130 g) sugar
1/2 cup (50 g) unsweetened cocoa powder
1 1/3 tbsp. (15 g) dextrose
1 1/2 tsp. (3.5 g) stabilizer for ice cream
1/3 oz. (10 g) 70% dark chocolate

METHOD

Pour the milk into a small saucepan and heat it to a temperature of about 115°F (45°C).
In the meanwhile, combine the sugar, the dextrose, the stabilizer and the unsweetened cocoa
powder. Slowly pour into the milk. Bring to 150°F (65°C) and then pasteurize at 185°F (85°C).
Add the dark chocolate, mix and quickly cool to 40°F (4°C) by putting the mixture into
a container immersed in a basin with water and ice. Allow to set at 40°F (4°C) for 6 hours.
Freeze by churning in an ice cream maker until the mixture is airy and dry in appearance,
i.e. not shiny (the time required depends on the ice cream maker used).
Transfer the ice cream into serving cups or cones, and serve.

Preparation time: 1 h - Resting time: 6 h
Difficulty: medium

GIANDUIA
OF TURIN
ICE CREAM

INGREDIENTS FOR ABOUT 4 1/2 CUPS (1 KG) OF ICE CREAM

4 cups (900 g) dark chocolate ice cream (recipe page 30)
1/2 cup (90 g) Piedmont hazelnut paste
2 1/2 tbsp. (45 g) acacia honey

METHOD

Using an immersion blender, carefully combine the chocolate ice cream
with the hazelnut paste and acacia honey.
Churn in an ice cream maker until the mixture is airy and dry in appearance, i.e. not shiny
(the time required depends on the ice cream maker used).
Transfer the Gianduia of Turin ice cream into individual cups or cones, and serve.

Preparation time: 1 h - Resting time: 6 h
Difficulty: medium

KIWI
ICE CREAM

INGREDIENTS FOR ABOUT 4 1/2 CUPS (1 KG) OF ICE CREAM

10 1/2 oz. (300 g) unpeeled kiwi fruit
1 1/3 cups (300 ml) water
1 cup (225 ml) whole milk
1 cup plus 3 tbsp. (225 g) sugar
juice of 1/4 lemon
1 1/2 tsp. (3.5 g) stabilizer for ice cream

METHOD

Peel the kiwi fruit and cut into pieces. You will need about 1 3/4 cups (250 g) of the kiwis.
Separately, combine the sugar and the stabilizer.
Using an immersion blender, blend the kiwi fruit with water while
slowly pouring in the dry ingredients. Add the lemon juice.
Allow to set at a temperature of 40°F (4°C) for 6 hours, add the milk and
churn in an ice cream maker until the mixture is airy and dry in appearance, i.e. not shiny
(the time required depends on the ice cream maker used).
You can place a slice of kiwi fruit at the bottom of some dessert bowls,
top with a spoonful of ice cream, and serve.

Preparation time: 20' - Resting time: 6 h
Difficulty: easy

MANGO ICE CREAM

INGREDIENTS FOR ABOUT 4 1/2 CUPS (1 KG) OF ICE CREAM

1/2 cup (100 ml) whole milk
1/2 cup (125 ml) water
2 3/4 cups (500 g) mango pulp
1 tbsp. (15 ml) lemon juice
1 cup (200 g) sugar
2 tbsp. (25 g) glucose
2 tsp. (4.5 g) stabilizer for ice cream

METHOD

In a small saucepan, heat milk and water to a temperature of 115°F (45°C).
Combine the sugar and the stabilizer, and slowly pour into the milk.
Then, add the glucose. Pasteurize at 185°F (85°C) and quickly cool to 40°F (4°C)
by putting the mixture into a container immersed in a basin with water and ice.
Add the mango pulp and allow to set at 40°F (4°C) for 6 hours. Then, add the lemon juice
and freeze by churning in an ice cream maker until the mixture is airy and dry in
appearance, i.e. not shiny (the time required depends on the ice cream maker used).
Transfer the mango ice cream into individual cups or cones
and garnish, if desired, with a few mango slices.

Preparation time: 1 h - Resting time: 6 h
Difficulty: easy

INGREDIENTS FOR ABOUT 4 1/2 CUPS (1 KG) OF ICE CREAM

1 1/3 cups (300 ml) whole milk
1/2 cup (100 ml) water
2 1/4 cups (400 g) melon pulp
3/4 cup (160 g) sugar
3 1/2 tbsp. (40 g) glucose
1 3/4 tbsp. (20 g) dextrose
2 1/3 tsp. (5 g) stabilizer for ice cream
2 tsp. (10 ml) lemon juice

METHOD

In a small saucepan, heat milk and water to a temperature of 115°F (45°C).
Separately, combine the sugar, the dextrose and the stabilizer, and slowly pour into the milk.
Add the glucose and pasteurize at 185°F (85°C). Quickly cool to 40°F (4°C)
by putting the mixture into a container immersed in a basin with water and ice.
Allow to set at 40°F (4°C) for 6 hours. Add the melon and lemon juice, and blend
everything together using an immersion blender. Churn in an ice cream maker
until the mixture is airy and dry in appearance, i.e. not shiny
(the time required depends on the ice cream maker used).
Transfer the melon ice cream into individual cups or cones.

Preparation time: 20' - Resting time: 6 h
Difficulty: easy

INGREDIENTS FOR ABOUT 4 CUPS (800 GRAMS) OF ICE CREAM

2 cups (500 ml) whole milk
2/3 cup (120 g) sugar
2 1/2 tbsp. (20 g) powdered skim milk
2 tbsp. (25 g) dextrose
1 1/2 tsp. (3.5 g) stabilizer for ice cream
1/3 cup (75 ml) cream
1/2 cup (90 g) pure pistachio paste

METHOD

In a small saucepan, heat the milk to a temperature of 115°F (45°C). Combine the sugar,
the powdered milk, the dextrose and the stabilizer, and slowly pour into the milk.
Bring to 150°F (65°C). Add the cream and pasteurize at 185°F (85°C).
Add the pistachio paste, carefully blend using an immersion blender and quickly cool to 40°F
(4°C) by putting the mixture into a container immersed in a basin with water and ice.
Allow to set at 40°F (4°C) for 6 hours and then freeze by churning
in an ice cream maker until the mixture is airy and dry in appearance,
i.e. not shiny (the time required depends on the ice cream maker used).
Transfer the pistachio ice cream into individual cups or cones.

Preparation time: 1 h - Resting time: 6 h
Difficulty: medium

NOUGAT ICE CREAM

INGREDIENTS FOR ABOUT 4 CUPS (800 GRAMS) OF ICE CREAM

2 cups (500 ml) whole milk
2/3 cup (120 g) sugar
2 1/2 tbsp. (20 g) skim milk powder
1 1/3 tbsp. (15 g) dextrose
1 1/2 tsp. (3.5 g) stabilizer for ice cream
1/3 cup (80 ml) cream
2 3/4 oz. (80 g) almond nougat

METHOD

In a small saucepan, heat the milk to a temperature of 115°F (45°C). Combine the sugar,
the powdered milk, the dextrose and the stabilizer, and slowly pour into the milk. Bring to 150°F
(65°C). Add the cream and pasteurize at 185°F (85°C). Then, quickly cool to 40°F (4°C)
by putting the mixture into a container immersed in a basin with water and ice.
Allow to set at 40°F (4°C) for 6 hours. Coarsely chop the almond nougat.
Churn the mixture in an ice cream maker. When the ice cream is almost ready,
incorporate the chopped nougat and continue to freeze
until the mixture is airy and dry in appearance, i.e. not shiny
(the time required depends on the ice cream maker used).
Transfer the nougat ice cream into individual cups or cones.

Preparation time: 1 h - Resting time: 6 h
Difficulty: medium

BANANA ICE CREAM

INGREDIENTS FOR ABOUT 4 1/2 CUPS (1 KG) OF ICE CREAM

1 2/3 cups (400 ml) whole milk
2 1/4 cups (400 g) pulp of ripe bananas
3/4 cup (160 g) sugar
3 1/2 tbsp. (40 g) glucose
1 3/4 tbsp. (20 g) dextrose
2 2/3 tsp. (6 g) stabilizer for ice cream

METHOD

In a small saucepan, heat milk to a temperature of 115°F (45°C).
Separately, combine the sugar, the dextrose and the stabilizer, and slowly pour into the milk.
Add the glucose and pasteurize at 185°F (85°C). Quickly cool to 40°F (4°C) by putting
the mixture into a container immersed in a basin with water and ice.
Allow to set at 40°F (4°C) for 6 hours, add the bananas and blend everything together
using an immersion blender. Then, freeze by churning in an ice cream maker
until the mixture is airy and dry in appearance, i.e. not shiny
(the time required depends on the ice cream maker used).
Transfer the banana ice cream into individual cups or cones.

Preparation time: 20' - Resting time: 6 h
Difficulty: easy

CHESTNUT
ICE CREAM

INGREDIENTS FOR ABOUT 4 1/2 CUPS (1 KG) OF ICE CREAM

2 1/4 cups (535 ml) whole milk
1 cup (150 g) dried chestnuts
1/2 cup (90 g) sugar
3 tbsp. (25 g) powdered skim milk
1 3/4 tbsp. (20 g) dextrose
1 tbsp. (6.5 g) stabilizer for ice cream
1/4 cup (65 ml) cream

METHOD

Soak the chestnuts in cold water for 12 hours. Drain, squeeze out any excess water
and boil in fresh water for about one hour, until they are well cooked. Allow them to cool and
pass through a vegetable mill. Weigh out about 1 1/2 cups (265 g). In a small saucepan, heat the
milk to a temperature of 115°F (45°C). Combine the sugar, powdered milk, dextrose and the
stabilizer, and slowly pour into the milk. Bring to 150°F (65°C). Add the cream and pasteurize at
185°F (85°C). Add the chestnut puree and quickly cool to 40°F (4°C) by putting the mixture into
a container immersed in a basin with water and ice. Allow to set at 40°F (4°C) for 6 hours. Freeze
by churning in an ice cream maker until the mixture is airy and dry in appearance,
i.e. not shiny (the time required depends on the ice cream maker used).
Transfer the chestnut ice cream into individual cups or cones.

Preparation time: 1 h 30' – Soaking time: 12 h
Resting time: 6 h - Difficulty: medium

CUSTARD
AND VANILLA
ICE CREAM

INGREDIENTS FOR ABOUT 4 CUPS (800 GRAMS) OF ICE CREAM (CUSTARD OR VANILLA)

2 cups (500 ml) whole milk
3 egg yolks
3/4 cup (150 g) sugar
1 3/4 tbsp. (20 g) dextrose
2 tbsp. (15 g) powdered skim milk

1 1/2 tsp. (3.5 g) stabilizer for ice cream
10 tbsp. (50 ml) cream
rind of half a lemon
one vanilla pod
3 coffee beans

METHOD

For the custard ice cream, heat milk with half of a vanilla pod split in two, coffee beans
and lemon rind peeled using a potato peeler (only the yellow portion) in a small saucepan to 115°F
(45°C). Combine the sugar, the powdered milk, the dextrose and the stabilizer, and slowly pour
into the milk. Bring to 150°F (65°C). Add the cream and egg yolks, and pasteurize at 185°F (85°C).
Quickly cool to 40°F (4°C) and allow to set for 6 hours. Then, filter the mixture using a colander
and freeze by churning in an ice cream maker until it is airy and dry in appearance,
i.e. not shiny (the time required depends on the ice cream maker used).
For the vanilla ice cream, omit the coffee beans and the lemon, and use an entire vanilla pod.
The pod should be cut with the point of a knife, the seeds scraped away with the edge
and added to the milk. Before churning, remove the pod but do not filter the seeds.

Preparation time: 1 h - Resting time: 6 h
Difficulty: medium

STRAWBERRY ICE CREAM

INGREDIENTS FOR ABOUT 4 1/2 CUPS (1 KG) OF ICE CREAM

1/2 cup (100 ml) whole milk
1 cup (245 ml) water
3 cups (450 g) strawberries
2 1/2 tsp. (12 ml) lemon juice
1 cup (230 g) sugar
2 1/3 tsp. (5 g) stabilizer for ice cream

METHOD

In a small saucepan, heat milk and water to a temperature of 115°F (45°C).
Combine the sugar and the stabilizer, and slowly pour into the milk.
Pasteurize at 185°F (85°C) and quickly cool to 40°F (4°C) by putting the mixture into
a container immersed in a basin with water and ice. Add the strawberries, washed, cleaned
and pureed with lemon juice, and allow the mixture to set at 40°F (4°C) for 6 hours.
Then, freeze by churning in an ice cream maker until the mixture is airy and dry in appearance,
i.e. not shiny (the time required depends on the ice cream maker used).
Transfer the strawberry ice cream into individual cups or cones.

Preparation time: 1 h - Resting time: 6 h
Difficulty: easy

ALMOND
ICE CREAM

INGREDIENTS FOR ABOUT 4 CUPS (850 GRAMS) OF ICE CREAM

2 cups (500 ml) whole milk
2/3 cup (120 g) sugar
2 1/2 tbsp. (20 g) powdered skim milk
1 3/4 tbsp. (20 g) dextrose

1 1/2 tsp. (3.5 g) stabilizer for ice cream
10 tbsp. (50 ml) cream
3/4 cup (100 g) sweet, blanched almonds
a few apricot kernels (optional)

METHOD

In a small saucepan, heat the milk to 115°F (45°C). Combine the sugar, the powdered milk,
the dextrose and the stabilizer, and slowly pour into the milk. Bring to 150°F (65°C).
Add the cream and pasteurize at 185°F (85°C). Quickly cool to 40°F (4°C) by putting the mixture
into a container immersed in a basin with water and ice. Allow to set at 40°F (4°C) for 6 hours.
Toast the sweet, blanched almonds in the oven set at 340°F (170°C) for a few minutes,
removing them as soon as they take on a bit of color. Allow to cool and grind
in an electric food processor until they are reduced to a very smooth paste.
For a more unique taste, you can add a few apricot kernels.
Add the paste to the mixture, blend using an immersion blender
and churn in an ice cream maker until it is airy and dry in appearance,
i.e. not shiny (the time required depends on the ice cream maker used).

Preparation time: 1 h - Resting time: 6 h
Difficulty: medium

INGREDIENTS FOR ABOUT 4 CUPS (800 GRAMS) OF ICE CREAM

2 cups (500 ml) whole milk
3 egg yolks
3/4 cup (150 g) sugar
2 tbsp. (25 g) dextrose
2 tbsp. (15 g) skim milk powder

1 1/2 tsp. (3.5 g) stabilizer for ice cream
rind of 1/4 lemon
1/4 vanilla pod
3 coffee beans
1/3 cup (80 g) Piedmont hazelnut paste

METHOD

In a small saucepan, heat the milk with the cut vanilla pod, coffee beans and lemon rind peeled using a potato peeler (only the yellow portion) to a temperature of 115°F (45°C). Combine the sugar, the powdered milk, the dextrose and the stabilizer, and slowly pour into the milk. Bring to 150°F (65°C). Add the egg yolks diluted with a small amount of the mixture, and pasteurize at 185°F (85°C). Filter the mixture using a colander, add the hazelnut paste and carefully blend using an immersion blender. Quickly cool to 40°F (4°C) by putting the mixture into a container immersed in a basin with water and ice. Allow to set at 40°F (4°C) for 6 hours and then freeze by churning in an ice cream maker until the mixture is airy and dry in appearance, i.e. not shiny (the time required depends on the ice cream maker used). Transfer the hazelnut ice cream into individual cups or cones.

Preparation time: 1 h - Resting time: 6 h
Difficulty: medium

YOGURT ICE CREAM

INGREDIENTS FOR ABOUT 4 1/2 CUPS (1 KG) OF ICE CREAM

1 1/2 cups (365 ml) whole milk
3/4 cup (165 g) sugar
3 1/2 tbsp. (28 g) skim milk powder
1 3/4 tbsp. (20 g) dextrose
2 1/3 tsp. (5 g) stabilizer for ice cream
1 2/3 cups (420 g) low-fat yogurt

METHOD

In a small saucepan, heat the milk to a temperature of 115°F (45°C).
Combine the sugar, the powdered milk, the dextrose and the stabilizer,
and slowly pour into the milk. Pasteurize at 185°F (85°C) and quickly cool to 40°F (4°C)
by putting the mixture into a container immersed in a basin with water and ice.
Allow to set at 40°F (4°C) for 6 hours and then add the yogurt.
Churn in an ice cream maker until the mixture is airy and dry in appearance,
i.e. not shiny (the time required depends on the ice cream maker used).
Transfer the yogurt ice cream into individual cups or cones.

Preparation time: 1 h - Resting time: 6 h
Difficulty: medium

ZABAGLIONE ICE CREAM

INGREDIENTS FOR ABOUT 4 1/2 CUPS (1 KG) OF ICE CREAM

1 1/2 cups (360 ml) whole milk
8 tsp. (40 ml) water
1 cup (250 ml) dry Marsala wine
8 egg yolks
1 cup (180 g) sugar
2 tbsp. (25 g) dextrose
2 tbsp. (15 g) powdered skim milk
2 1/3 tsp. (5 g) stabilizer for ice cream

METHOD

In a small saucepan, boil the Marsala for 2 minutes (be careful not to catch it on fire) and then add the water and the milk. Combine the sugar, the powdered milk, the dextrose and the stabilizer, and slowly pour into the liquid mixture. Dilute the egg yolks with a small amount of the liquid, add to the saucepan and pasteurize at a temperature of 185°F (85°C). Quickly cool to 40°F (4°C) by putting the mixture into a container immersed in a basin with water and ice.
Allow to set at 40°F (4°C) for 6 hours and then freeze by churning in an ice cream maker until the mixture is airy and dry in appearance, i.e. not shiny
(the time required depends on the ice cream maker used).
Transfer the zabaglione ice cream into individual cups or cones.

Preparation time: 1 h - Resting time: 6 h
Difficulty: medium

INGREDIENTS FOR ABOUT 3 1/2 CUPS (750 GRAMS) OF ICE CREAM

2 cups (500 ml) whole milk
2/3 cup (120 g) sugar
2 1/2 tbsp. (20 g) powdered skim milk
1 1/3 tbsp. (15 g) dextrose
1 1/2 tsp. (3.5 g) stabilizer for ice cream
1/3 cup (75 ml) cream
2 1/2 tbsp. (30 g) Arabica coffee beans

METHOD

First steep the coffee in cold milk for 12 hours.
Filter and pour the milk into a small saucepan and bring to a temperature of about 115°F (45°C).
Combine the sugar, the powdered milk, the dextrose and the stabilizer, and slowly pour into the milk. Bring to 150°F (65°C). Add the cream and pasteurize at 185°F (85°C). Quickly cool to 40°F (4°C) by putting the mixture into a container immersed in a basin with water and ice.
Allow to set at 40°F (4°C) for 6 hours.
Freeze by churning in an ice cream maker until the mixture is airy and dry in appearance, i.e. not shiny (the time required depends on the ice cream maker used).
Transfer the white coffee ice cream into individual cups or cones, and serve.

Preparation time: 1 h – Steeping time: 12 h
Resting time: 6 h - Difficulty: medium

STRACCIATELLA ICE CREAM

**INGREDIENTS FOR ABOUT 4 CUPS (800 GRAMS)
OF ICE CREAM (FIORDILATTE OR STRACCIATELLA)**

For the fiordilatte ice cream
2 cups (500 ml) whole milk
2/3 cup (120 g) sugar
2 1/2 tbsp. (20 g) powdered skim milk
1 1/3 tbsp. (15 g) dextrose

1 1/2 tsp. (3.5 g) stabilizer for ice cream
1/2 cup (125 ml) cream

For the stracciatella ice cream
3 oz. (90 g) dark chocolate, chopped

METHOD

For the fiordilatte ice cream, pour the milk into a small saucepan, and bring it to a temperature of 115°F (45°C). Combine the sugar, the powdered milk, the dextrose and the stabilizer, and slowly pour into the milk. Bring to 150°F (65°C). Add the cream and pasteurize at 185°F (85°C). Quickly cool to 40°F (4°C) by putting the mixture into a container immersed in a basin with water and ice. Allow to set at 40°F (4°C) for 6 hours.
Freeze by churning in an ice cream maker until the mixture is airy and dry in appearance, i.e. not shiny (the time required depends on the ice cream maker used).
If you wish to make the stracciatella ice cream, simply mix the chopped dark chocolate with freshly made fiordilatte ice cream. Transfer the fiordilatte (or stracciatella) ice cream into individual cups or cones, and serve.

Preparation time: 1 h - Resting time: 6 h
Difficulty: medium

INGREDIENTS FOR ABOUT 4 1/2 CUPS (1 KG) OF ICE CREAM

For the custard ice cream
2 cups (500 ml) whole milk
3 egg yolks
3/4 cup (150 g) sugar
1 3/4 tbsp. (20 g) dextrose
2 tbsp. (15 g) powdered skim milk

1 1/2 tsp. (3.5 g) stabilizer
for ice cream
10 tbsp. (50 ml) cream
rind of half a lemon
half a vanilla pod
3 coffee beans

For the sour cherry swirling
1 2/3 cups (250 g) sour cherries,
pitted
juice of 1/4 lemon
3/4 cup (150 g) sugar
3 tbsp. (30 g) cornstarch

64

METHOD

For the swirling, bring the sour cherries and lemon juice to a boil in a small saucepan.
Add the sugar mixed with cornstarch and boil for a couple of minutes. Allow to cool.
For the custard ice cream, heat milk with the split half of a vanilla pod, coffee beans and lemon rind peeled using a potato peeler (only the yellow portion) in a small saucepan to 115°F (45°C). Combine the sugar, the powdered milk, the dextrose and the stabilizer, and slowly pour into the milk. Bring to 150°F (65°C). Add the cream and egg yolks, and pasteurize at 185°F (85°C). Quickly cool to 40°F (4°C) by putting the mixture into a container immersed in a basin with water and ice. Allow to set at 40°F (4°C) for 6 hours, filter the mixture using a colander and then freeze by churning in an ice cream maker until the mixture is airy and dry in appearance, i.e. not shiny (the time required depends on the ice cream maker used).
Swirl the ice cream with the cherry sauce, setting some aside to use as a garnish.

Preparation time: 1 h - Resting time: 6 h
Difficulty: medium

SORBETS, ITALIAN ICES AND POPSICLES

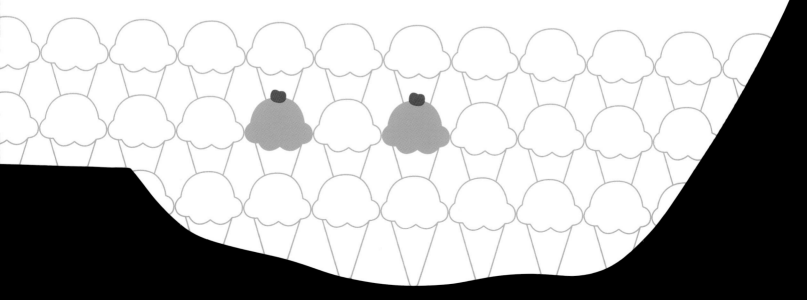

INGREDIENTS FOR 4 POPSICLES

1 cup (200 ml) water
1/4 cup (45 g) sugar
1 tsp. (5 g) dextrose
1/3 cup (70 ml) lemon juice

68

METHOD

Allow the sugar and dextrose to dissolve in unheated water,
and then add lemon juice filtered through a strainer.
Pour into popsicle molds and insert the sticks.
Place into the freezer for two to four hours, until frozen.
If desired, you can add thin lemon slices to the molds before inserting the popsicle sticks.

Preparation time: 15' - Setting time: 2-4 h
Difficulty: easy

INGREDIENTS FOR 6 POPSICLES

1 cup (220 ml) water
3 tbsp. (40 g) brown sugar
1/3 cup (80 ml) lime juice
8 tsp. (40 ml) Rum
fresh mint

METHOD

Allow the sugar to dissolve in unheated water, and then add lemon
juice filtered through a strainer.
Mix in the Rum and add some fresh mint leaves,
washed, dried and torn into pieces.
Pour into popsicle molds (you can also just use disposable
plastic cups) and insert the sticks.
Place into the freezer until frozen, for 2-4 hours.

Preparation time: 15' - Setting time: 2-4 h
Difficulty: easy

COFFEE
ITALIAN ICE

INGREDIENTS FOR 2 GENEROUS CUPS (500 GRAMS) OF ITALIAN ICE

2/3 cup (150 ml) espresso coffee
1 cup (255 ml) water
1/2 cup (100 g) sugar

METHOD

Dissolve the sugar in hot coffee and then add water. Allow to cool.
Transfer everything into a bowl and place in the freezer.
Every so often, stir the Italian ice with a whisk, breaking up the section that
begins to freeze. Continue to do so until the entire mixture
transforms into a homogeneous Italian ice.
Remove from the freezer and serve in individual cups.

Preparation time: 15' - Setting time: 2-4 h
Difficulty: easy

ALMOND MILK
ITALIAN ICE

INGREDIENTS FOR 2 GENEROUS CUPS (500 GRAMS) OF ITALIAN ICE

1 1/2 cups (200 g) almonds
2 1/2 cups (600 ml) water
1/3 cup (70 g) sugar
1 tbsp. (12 g) dextrose

METHOD

Finely grind the almonds and combine with the water. Place into the refrigerator
for a few hours then transfer to a clean cloth and wring to obtain almond milk.
Dissolve the sugar and dextrose in the unheated almond milk.
Place the liquid into the freezer until it begins to freeze.
Every so often, mix well using a whisk and replace in the freezer.
Repeat this procedure at least 4-5 times before the Italian ice is ready
(it will take 2 to 4 hours).
Take out of the freezer and serve the almond milk Italian ice in individual glasses.

Preparation time: 15' - Resting time: 8 h - Setting time: 2-4 h
Difficulty: easy

INGREDIENTS FOR 2 GENEROUS CUPS (500 GRAMS) OF ITALIAN ICE

1 2/3 cups (400 ml) water
3 tbsp. (40 g) sugar
1/2 cup (100 ml) mint syrup

For the decoration
fresh mint leaves (optional)

METHOD

Prepare the sugar syrup by boiling water with sugar for one minute.
Allow to cool and add the mint syrup.
Place the liquid into the freezer until it begins to freeze.
Every so often, mix well using a whisk and replace in the freezer.
Repeat this procedure at least 4-5 times before the Italian ice is ready.
Take out of the freezer and serve in individual cups garnishing, if desired,
with washed and dried fresh mint leaves.

Preparation time: 15' - Setting time: 2-4 h
Difficulty: easy

INGREDIENTS FOR ABOUT 4 1/2 CUPS (1 KG) OF SORBET

2 cups (485 ml) water
1 cup (210 ml) lemon juice
1 cup (210 g) sugar
3 1/2 tbsp. (40 g) glucose powder
1 1/3 tbsp. (15 g) dextrose
1 tbsp. plus 2/3 tsp. (8 g) stabilizer for ice cream

METHOD

Combine the sugar, the glucose powder, the dextrose and the stabilizer.
Slowly pour into boiling water and bring to a temperature of 150°F (65°C),
whisking continuously.
Allow to cool and then set at 40°F (4°C) for 6 hours.
Add lemon juice and pour into an ice cream maker. Churn until the mixture is dry
and clump-free in appearance (the time required depends on the ice cream maker used).
Transfer the lemon sorbet into serving cups.

Preparation time: 30' - Resting time: 6 h
Difficulty: easy

MOSCATO D'ASTI SORBET

INGREDIENTS FOR ABOUT 4 1/2 CUPS (1 KG) OF SORBET

1 cup (225 ml) water
1 cup plus 3 tbsp. (240 g) sugar
2 tbsp. plus 1 tsp. (35 ml) glucose syrup
2 1/3 tsp. (5 g) stabilizer for ice cream
2 cups (500 ml) Moscato d'Asti wine DOCG

METHOD

Combine the sugar and the stabilizer.
Slowly pour into boiling water. Add the glucose syrup
and bring to a temperature of 150°F (65°C), whisking continuously.
Allow to cool and then set at 40°F (4°C) for 6 hours.
Add Moscato d'Asti wine and pour into an ice cream maker. Churn until the mixture is dry
and clump-free in appearance (the time required depends on the ice cream maker used).
Transfer the Moscato d'Asti sorbet into serving cups.

Preparation time: 30' - Resting time: 6 h
Difficulty: easy

INGREDIENTS FOR ABOUT 4 1/2 CUPS (1 KG) OF SORBET

1 cup (235 ml) water
1 1/3 cups (270 g) sugar
8 tsp. (40 ml) glucose syrup
1 1/3 tsp. (3 g) stabilizer for ice cream
2 cups (460 ml) pink grapefruit juice (about 5 grapefruits)
2 tsp. (10 ml) lemon juice

METHOD

Combine the sugar and the stabilizer.
Slowly pour into boiling water. Add the glucose syrup
and bring to a temperature of 150°F (65°C), whisking continuously.
Allow to cool and then set at 40°F (4°C) for 6 hours.
Add the lemon and pink grapefruit juices and pour into an ice cream maker.
Churn until the mixture is dry and clump-free in appearance
(the time required depends on the ice cream maker used).
Transfer the pink grapefruit sorbet into serving cups.

Preparation time: 30' - Resting time: 6 h
Difficulty: easy

PINEAPPLE SORBET

INGREDIENTS FOR ABOUT 4 1/2 CUPS (1 KG) OF SORBET

1 cup plus 3 tbsp. (280 ml) water
1/2 cup (100 g) sugar
4 tbsp. (45 g) dextrose
1 tbsp. (16 ml) glucose syrup
2 tsp. (4.5 g) stabilizer for ice cream
3 cups (540 g) pineapple pulp
1 tbsp. (15 ml) lemon juice

METHOD

Combine the sugar, the dextrose and the stabilizer.
Slowly pour into boiling water. Add the glucose syrup
and bring to a temperature of 150°F (65°C), whisking continuously.
Allow to cool and then set at 40°F (4°C) for 6 hours.
Add the lemon juice and pineapple pulp. Blend together using an immersion blender.
Pour into an ice cream maker and churn until the mixture is dry and clump-free
in appearance (the time required depends on the ice cream maker used).
Transfer the pineapple sorbet into serving cups.

Preparation time: 30' - Resting time: 6 h
Difficulty: easy

STRAWBERRY SORBET

INGREDIENTS FOR ABOUT 4 CUPS (800 GRAMS) OF STRAWBERRY SORBET

2 cups (300 g) strawberries
1 1/3 cups (300 ml) water
1 cup (200 g) sugar
1 1/3 tbsp. (15 g) dextrose
juice of 1/4 lemon
1 3/4 tsp. (4 g) stabilizer for ice cream

METHOD

Carefully wash, delicately dry and cut the strawberries.
Separately, combine the sugar, the dextrose and the stabilizer. Blend the strawberries
with water while slowly pouring in the dry ingredients. Add the lemon juice.
Allow to set at a temperature of 40°F (4°C) for 6 hours and then freeze
in an ice cream maker until the mixture is dry and clump-free in appearance
(the time required depends on the ice cream maker used).
Transfer the strawberry sorbet into individual cups or cones.

Preparation time: 20' - Resting time: 6 h
Difficulty: easy

CAKES, SUNDAES AND SNACKS

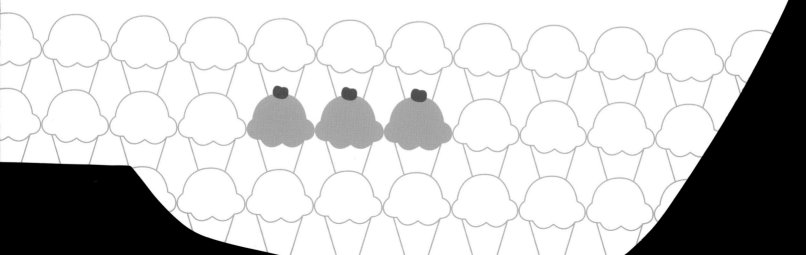

INGREDIENTS FOR 4 SUNDAES

4 bananas
2/3 cup (150 g) vanilla
ice cream (recipe page 48)
2/3 cup (150 g) strawberry ice
cream (recipe page 50)

2/3 cup (150 g) dark chocolate
ice cream (recipe page 30)

For the chocolate sauce
8 tsp. (40 ml) cream

1 tsp. (5 g) glucose (optional)
1 1/2 oz. (40 g) dark chocolate

For the decoration
1 cup (120 g) sweetened
whipped cream

90

METHOD

To prepare the chocolate sauce, boil the cream with the glucose (if used)
and pour it over the chopped dark chocolate. Carefully mix using a soft spatula
until the sauce is smooth and velvety.
In some oval serving bowls (it is best to let them first cool in the freezer),
place two halves of a banana cut lengthwise (this should be done on the spot to prevent
oxidation of the fruit) and position a ball of each of the three ice cream flavors between them.
Garnish with whipped cream using a star-tipped pastry bag
and then with the chocolate sauce
(warming it up in a bain-marie or in the microwave if necessary).

Preparation time: 10'
Difficulty: easy

CAPPUCCINO ICE CREAM SANDWICHES

INGREDIENTS FOR ABOUT 15 ICE CREAM SANDWICHES

For the ice cream
2 cups (500 ml) whole milk
2/3 cup (120 g) sugar
2 1/2 tbsp. (20 g) powdered skim milk
1 1/3 tbsp. (15 g) dextrose

1 1/2 tsp. (3.5 g) stabilizer
1/3 cup (80 ml) cream
3 tsp. (5 g) instant coffee

For the chocolate cookies
2 cups (250 g) flour

2/3 cup (140 g) butter
2/3 cup (125 g) sugar
3 egg yolks
2 tbsp. (15 g) unsweetened cocoa powder
a pinch of salt

METHOD

For the cookies, cream together room temperature butter with sugar on a pastry board and then incorporate a pinch of salt and the egg yolks. Add flour sifted with unsweetened cocoa powder and briefly knead until the dough is thoroughly combined. Wrap the dough in plastic wrap and place in the refrigerator to rest for at least one hour. Roll out the dough on a floured pastry board using a rolling pin to a thickness of about 1/8 of an inch (3 mm). Use a cookie cutter to cut out disks about 2 inches (6 cm) in diameter. Arrange on a baking sheet lined with parchment paper and bake at 350°F (180°C) for about 15 minutes. For the ice cream, heat the milk in a small saucepan to 115°F (45°C). Combine the sugar, the powdered milk, the dextrose and the stabilizer, and slowly pour into the milk. Bring to 150°F (65°C). Add the cream and pasteurize at 185°F (85°C). Add instant coffee to the boiling mixture and then quickly cool to 40°F (4°C). Allow to set at 40°F (4°C) for 6 hours. Churn the mixture in an ice cream maker (the time required depends on the ice cream maker used). Sandwich the ice cream between pairs of pre-cooled cookies and store in the freezer.

Preparation time: 1 h 30' - Cooking time: 15' - Resting time: 6 h
Difficulty: medium

CUSTARD AND CHOCOLATE ICE CREAM SANDWICHES

INGREDIENTS FOR ABOUT 15 ICE CREAM SANDWICHES

2 cups (450 g) custard ice cream
(recipe page 48)
2 cups (450 g) dark chocolate
ice cream (recipe page 30)

For the cocoa shortcrust pastry
2 cups (250 g) flour

2/3 cup (140 g) butter
2/3 cup (125 g) sugar
3 egg yolks
2 tbsp. (15 g) unsweetened
cocoa powder
a pinch of salt

For the vanilla shortcrust pastry
1 cup (125 g) flour
1/3 cup (75 g) butter
1/3 cup (65 g) sugar
2 egg yolks
a pinch of vanilla powder
a pinch of salt

METHOD

For the shortcrust pastry, work together room temperature butter with the sugar on a pastry board and then incorporate a pinch of salt and the egg yolks. Add flour sifted with vanilla powder and briefly knead until the dough is homogeneous. Wrap the dough in plastic wrap and place in the refrigerator to rest for at least one hour before use. For the cocoa shortcrust pastry, follow the same procedure but sift the flour with the cocoa instead of the vanilla powder. Roll out the two doughs on a floured pastry board using a rolling pin to a thickness of about 1/8 of an inch (3 mm) and cut out square cookies about 2x3 inches (6x7 cm) in size or any other desired shape. Arrange on a baking sheet lined with parchment paper and bake at 350°F (180°C) for about 15 minutes. Sandwich the two ice cream flavours between pairs of pre-cooled cookies and store in the freezer until consumption.

Preparation time: 1 h 30' - Cooking time: 15' - Resting time: 6 h
Difficulty: medium

THREE-COLORED BOMB CAKE

INGREDIENTS FOR 6-8 PEOPLE

For the ice cream
1 1/2 cups (300 g) custard ice cream (recipe page 48)
1 1/2 cups (300 g) dark chocolate ice cream
(recipe page 30)
1 1/2 cups (300 g) hazelnut ice cream (recipe page 54)

For the chocolate cookie
1 egg white
2 1/2 tbsp. (30 g) granulated sugar
1 egg yolk
1 1/2 tbsp. (10 g) cocoa powder

METHOD

For the cookie, beat the egg white with the sugar, delicately combine with the egg yolk and then add the cocoa powder. Form the cookie using a pastry bag on a baking sheet lined with parchment paper and bake at 320°F (160°C) for about 15 minutes. Take three, semi-spherical metal nesting molds, the largest about 7 inches (18 cm) in diameter. Fill the smallest completely with custard ice cream and smooth using a spatula. Place in the freezer for at least one hour then extract the ice cream by passing the mold under cold water. Replace the ice cream dome in the freezer. Coat the inside of the medium size mold (stored in the freezer) with a layer of chocolate ice cream and insert the custard dome. Smooth with a spatula and place in the freezer for at least one hour. Then, extract from the mold and replace in the freezer. Coat the interior of the largest dome with a layer of hazelnut ice cream and insert the custard and chocolate dome. Cover with the chocolate cookie and replace in the freezer for at least one hour. Extract from the mold and decorate as desired.

Preparation time: 1 h - Cooking time: 15' - Setting time: 3 h
Difficulty: high

ICE CREAM CASSATA

INGREDIENTS FOR 4 CASSATA

2/3 cup (150 g) pistachio ice cream (recipe page 40)
2/3 cup (150 g) dark chocolate ice cream (recipe page 30)
1 cup (250 g) fiordilatte ice cream (recipe page 62)
1/4 cup (50 g) candied citron and orange, diced

METHOD

Coat the interior of suitable metal molds with a layer of pistachio ice cream.
Allow to harden in the freezer for at least half an hour and then repeat
the same process using dark chocolate ice cream.
Allow to harden in the freezer for at least half an hour
and fill with fiordilatte ice cream mixed with finely diced candied fruit.
Place the ice cream cassatas in the freezer again until completely hardened,
at least half an hour. Extract by passing the molds under cold water for a few seconds.

Preparation time: 1 h - Setting time: 1 h 30'
Difficulty: medium

AMARETTO
ICE CREAM CONES

INGREDIENTS FOR ABOUT 10 ICE CREAM CONES

10 cones

For the amaretto ice cream
2 cups (500 ml) whole milk
2/3 cup (125 g) sugar

2 1/2 tbsp. (20 g) powdered skim milk
1 1/2 tsp. (3.5 g) stabilizer
1/2 cup (125 ml) cream
2 tsp. (10 ml) Amaretto liqueur
7 oz. (200 g) amaretti cookies

For the decoration
5 1/4 oz. (150 g) milk chocolate
10 mini amaretti cookies
3 tbsp. (20 g) toasted almond slices

METHOD

In a small saucepan, heat the milk to 115°F (45°C). Combine the sugar, the powdered milk and the stabilizer, and slowly pour into the milk. Bring to 150°F (65°C). Add the cream and pasteurize at 185°F (85°C). Quickly cool to 40°F (4°C) and allow to set at 40°F (4°C) for 6 hours. Add the liqueur and freeze by churning in an ice cream maker until the mixture is airy and dry in appearance, i.e. not shiny (the time required depends on the ice cream maker used). When the ice cream is almost ready, add the crumbled amaretti cookies. Fill ten truncated cone silicon molds, 2 1/4 x 2 inches (6x5 cm) at the base, using a small spatula or a pastry bag. Place in the freezer to harden for one hour. Extract from the molds and replace in the freezer. Melt the chocolate by bringing it to about 115°F (45°C) and then cool to 90°F (32°C) while mixing. Dip the tops of the cones into the chocolate, allow to drain and insert a cone of ice cream into each. Place into the freezer for a few minutes and, working quickly, dip the tops of the cones into the chocolate. Drain excess chocolate and sprinkle with almond slices. Top with a mini amaretto cookie.

Preparation time: 1 h - Resting time: 6 h - Setting time: 1 h
Difficulty: medium

CHOCOLATE ICE CREAM CONES WITH SOUR CHERRIES

INGREDIENTS FOR ABOUT 10 ICE CREAM CONES

10 cones
2 3/4 cups (600 g) fiordilatte ice cream
(recipe page 62)
2 3/4 cups (600 g) dark chocolate ice
cream (recipe page 30)

For the decoration
5 1/4 oz. (150 g) dark chocolate
multicolored sprinkles
40-50 sour cherries in syrup

METHOD

To prepare the coating, melt the chocolate by bringing it to about 115°F (45°C),
then cool to 90°F (32°C) while mixing.
Dip the tops of the cones into the chocolate, allow excess chocolate to drain
and sprinkle with cylinder sprinkles.
Spoon the two ice cream flavors into two disposable pastry bags and
fill the cones alternating the flavors.
As you are filling, also add some sour cherries, drained of their syrup.
Place the cones into a cone holder and put into the freezer
to harden for at least half an hour.
Take out the cones and garnish with the remaining sour cherries.

Preparation time: 1 h - Resting time: 6 h - Setting time: 30'
Difficulty: medium

INGREDIENTS FOR ABOUT 6 ICE CREAM CONES

6 cones

For the praline ice cream
2 cups (500 ml) whole milk
3 egg yolks
3/4 cup (150 g) sugar
2 tbsp. (25 g) dextrose

2 tbsp. (15 g) skim milk powder
1 1/2 tsp. (3.5 g) stabilizer

For the pralinated hazelnut paste
1/2 cup (70 g) toasted hazelnuts
1/4 cup (50 g) sugar
2 tsp. (10 ml) water

For the dark chocolate coating
4 1/2 oz. (125 g) dark chocolate
3 tbsp. (40 g) cocoa butter

For the decoration
1/3 cup (50 g) pralinated
chopped hazelnuts

METHOD

In a small saucepan, caramelize the sugar with water. Add the hazelnuts and cook until they take on a slightly darker color. Transfer to an oiled tray. Allow to cool and grind in an electric food processor until they form a paste. Heat the milk to 115°F (45°C). Combine the sugar, the powdered milk, the dextrose and the stabilizer, and slowly pour into the milk. Bring to 150°F (65°C). Add the egg yolks diluted with a small amount of the mixture, and pasteurize at 185°F (85°C). Add the pralinated hazelnut paste, carefully mix and quickly cool to 40°F (4°C). Allow to set at 40°F (4°C) for 6 hours and then churn in an ice cream maker. Fill six semi-spherical silicon molds and cones with ice cream. Turn the cones upside down and insert into the molds. Allow to harden for at least one hour. Melt the chocolate and cocoa butter by bringing them to about 115°F (45°C) then cool to 90°F (32°C) while mixing. Extract the cones from the molds, dip the tops into the chocolate, drain the excess and sprinkle with chopped hazelnuts.

Preparation time: 1 h - Resting time: 6 h - Setting time: 1 h
Difficulty: high

CHOCOLATE COATED MINT ICE CREAM BARS

INGREDIENTS FOR ABOUT 10 BARS

For the mint swirl ice cream
2 cups (500 ml) whole milk
2/3 cup (120 g) sugar
2 1/2 tbsp. (20 g) powdered skim milk
1 1/3 tbsp. (15 g) dextrose

1 1/2 tsp. (3.5 g) stabilizer
1/2 cup (125 ml) cream
mint extract

For the swirling
1/4 cup (60 ml) green mint syrup

For the dark chocolate coating
7 oz. (200 g) dark chocolate
1/3 cup (65 g) cocoa butter
edible gold flakes

METHOD

In a small saucepan, heat the milk to 115°F (45°C). Combine the sugar, the powdered milk, the dextrose and the stabilizer, and slowly pour into the milk. Bring to 150°F (65°C). Add the cream and pasteurize at 185°F (85°C). Add the mint extract and quickly cool to 40°F (4°C).
Allow to set at 40°F (4°C) for 6 hours and then freeze by churning in an ice cream maker.
As soon as the ice cream is ready, swirl with the mint syrup. Fill an ice cream bar mold or simple plastic cups with the ice cream using a pastry bag and insert wooden ice cream sticks.
Place into the freezer to harden for at least two hours. For the coating,
melt the chocolate and the cocoa butter by bringing them to about 115°F (45°C),
then cool to 90°F (32°C) while mixing. Extract the bars and, working rather quickly,
dip them into the coating, allow excess chocolate to drain and sprinkle with edible
gold flakes, if desired. Place in the freezer for a few minutes before serving.

Preparation time: 1 h - Resting time: 6 h - Setting time: 2 h
Difficulty: medium

HAZELNUT ICE CREAM BARS

INGREDIENTS FOR ABOUT 10 BARS

3 1/4 cups (700 g) hazelnut ice cream (recipe page 54)

For the dark chocolate coating
9 oz. (250 g) dark chocolate
1/2 cup (80 g) cocoa butter

For the decoration
3/4 cup (100 g) toasted hazelnuts

METHOD
Fill a silicon ice cream bar mold with hazelnut ice cream using a pastry bag.
Then, insert the ice cream sticks and level using a spatula.
Place into the freezer to harden for at least two hours.
Coarsely chop the toasted hazelnuts and set aside.
For the dark chocolate coating, melt the chocolate and the cocoa butter by bringing
them to a temperature of about 115°F (45°C), then cool to 90°F (32°C) while mixing.
Extract the bars and, working rather quickly, dip them into the coating,
allow excess chocolate to drain and sprinkle with the hazelnuts.
Place the ice cream bars in the freezer for a few minutes before serving.

Preparation time: 30' - Resting time: 2 h
Difficulty: medium

MILK CHOCOLATE COATED VANILLA ICE CREAM BARS

INGREDIENTS FOR ABOUT 10 BARS

3 1/4 cups (700 g) vanilla ice cream (recipe page 48)

For the milk chocolate coating
9 oz. (250 g) milk chocolate
1/2 cup (100 g) cocoa butter

For the decoration
1 3/4 oz. (50 g) dark chocolate

METHOD

Fill a silicon ice cream bar mold with vanilla ice cream using a pastry bag. Then, insert the ice cream sticks and level using a spatula. Place into the freezer to harden for at least two hours.
For the milk chocolate coating, melt the chocolate and the cocoa butter by bringing them to a temperature of about 115°F (45°C), then cool to 90°F (32°C) while mixing.
Follow the same procedure for the dark chocolate coating: melt it by bringing it to a temperature of about 115°F (45°C), then cool to 90°F (32°C) while mixing. Take the bars out of their molds and, working rather quickly, dip them into the milk chocolate coating, allow the excess chocolate to drain and drizzle with dark chocolate using a paper piping cone.
Place in the freezer for a few minutes before serving.

Preparation time: 30' - Resting time: 2 h
Difficulty: medium

STRAWBERRY MERINGUE CAKE

INGREDIENTS FOR 4-6 PEOPLE

For the meringue disks
3 egg whites
1 cup (180 g) sugar
2 tbsp. (18 g) cornstarch (optional)
1 2/3 cups (350 g) strawberry ice cream
(recipe page 50)

For the decoration
2 2/3 cups (300 g) sweetened whipped cream
1 cup (150 g) strawberries
chopped pistachios

112

METHOD

For the meringue disks, beat the egg whites adding some sugar half way through.
Incorporate the remaining sugar (mixed with the cornstarch, if used) at the end by hand.
Form two meringue disks approximately 7-8 inches (18-20 cm) in diameter and a few small
meringues with the remaining mixture on baking sheets lined with parchment paper.
Bake at 210°F (100°C) for about 3 hours with the vent open (or the oven door slightly ajar).
Store in a dry location before use.
Arrange the strawberry ice cream on the first meringue disk using an ice cream scooper.
Cover with the second disk pressing down lightly. Store in the freezer until consumption.
Right before serving, garnish the meringue cake with whipped cream using
a star-tipped pastry bag. Decorate the dessert with fresh strawberries,
some meringue pieces and chopped pistachios.

Preparation time: 30' - Cooking time: 3 h
Difficulty: high

BELLA ELENA
PEARS

INGREDIENTS FOR 4 SUNDAES

1 cup (250 g) vanilla ice cream
(recipe page 48)

For the poached pears
4 small, firm pears
2/3 cup (120 g) sugar

one vanilla pod
1 cup (200 ml) water

For the chocolate sauce
1/3 cup (80 ml) cream
2 1/2 tsp. (10 g) glucose (optional)

3 oz. (80 g) dark chocolate

For the decoration
1 cup (120 g) whipped cream
1 1/2 tbsp. (10 g) toasted almond
slices

METHOD

Prepare the vanilla syrup by melting the sugar in a saucepan wih water and boiling with the
vanilla pod for about 2 minutes. Peel the pears, cut them into halves and remove the cores.
Add the pears to the syrup. Simmer for 1-2 minutes then turn off the heat and allow to cool.
As an alternative, you can use pears canned in syrup.
For the chocolate sauce, add the glucose (if used) to the cream, bring to a boil and pour over
the chopped chocolate. Carefully stir using a soft spatula until the sauce is smooth and velvety.
In each serving bowl (it is best to let them first cool in the freezer), place a scoop of ice cream,
arrange two syrup-poached pear halves and top with a little bit of whipped cream
using a star-tipped pastry bag. Garnish with the chocolate sauce (warm it up
in a bain-marie or in the microwave if necessary) and the almond slices.

Preparation time: 30' - Resting time: 2 h
Difficulty: medium

PEACH MELBA

INGREDIENTS FOR 4 SUNDAES

1 cup (250 g) vanilla ice cream
(recipe page 48)

For the syruped peaches
2 firm, yellow peaches
2/3 cup (120 g) sugar

one vanilla pod
1 cup (200 ml) water

For the raspberry sauce
1/2 cup (60 g) raspberries
2 tbsp. (25 g) sugar

a few drops of lemon juice

For the decoration
1 1/2 cups (180 g) whipped cream
1 1/2 tbsp. (10 g) toasted almond
slices

METHOD

Drop the peaches for 30 seconds into a saucepan of boiling water, drain using a slotted spoon,
and cool in a mixture of water and ice, which will allow the skin to be easily removed.
Split into halves and remove the pits. In the meanwhile, prepare the syrup by melting
the sugar in a saucepan with water and boiling with the vanilla pod for about 2 minutes.
Pour the syrup over the peaches and allow to marinate for 12 hours.
As an alternative, you can use peaches canned in syrup.
For the sauce, blend the raspberries with sugar and lemon juice using an immersion
blender and pass through a sieve. In each serving bowl (it is best to let them first cool
in the freezer), place a scoop of vanilla ice cream, cover it with a syruped peach
half and distribute some whipped cream dabs on top and around.
Garnish with the raspberry sauce and the almond slices.

Preparation time: 30' - Resting time: 12 h
Difficulty: medium

116

FROZEN TRUFFLE

INGREDIENTS FOR 4-6 TRUFFLES

1 1/2 cups (315 g) dark chocolate ice cream mixture (recipe page 30)
1 1/2 cups (315 g) vanilla ice cream mixture (recipe page 48)
4 1/2 tbsp. (65 g) hazelnut paste
2/3 cup (150 g) dark chocolate ice cream (recipe page 30)
1/4 cup (30 g) chopped hazelnuts
unsweetened cocoa powder

METHOD

Mix the chocolate and vanilla ice cream mixtures with hazelnut paste
and churn in an ice cream maker until the mixture is airy and dry in appearance,
i.e. not shiny (the time required depends on the ice cream maker used).
Coat the interior of suitable metal molds, kept in the freezer,
with a layer of the resulting ice cream.
Sprinkle with chopped hazelnuts and finish with a ball of chocolate
ice cream scooped using an ice cream scooper.
Smooth using a spatula and place in the freezer for at least one hour.
Extract the truffles by passing the molds under cold water
and then dip into a bowl of cocoa powder.

Preparation time: 40' - Setting time: 1 h
Difficulty: easy

PISTACHIO ICE CREAM
CAKE WITH SOUR CHERRIES

INGREDIENTS FOR 6-8 PEOPLE

2 cups (450 g) fiordilatte ice
cream (recipe page 62)
2 cups (450 g) pistachio ice
cream (recipe page 40)
10 sour cherries in syrup

For the almond meringue disk
1/3 cup (50 g) icing sugar
1/3 cup (50 g) unblanched almonds
2 egg whites
1 1/2 tbsp. (20 g) granulated sugar

For the decoration
10 sour cherries in syrup
1/3 cup (50 g) peeled pistachios
1/3 cup (65 g) sugar
4 tsp. (20 ml) water

METHOD

For the almond meringue disk, grind icing sugar with almonds in a food processor. Delicately incorporate the resulting mixture into egg whites whipped with the 1 1/2 tablespoons (20 g) of granulated sugar. Shape a meringue disk approximately 6 inches (16 cm) in diameter using a pastry bag and a strip approximately 1x8 inches (3x20 cm) in size on a baking sheet lined with parchment paper. Bake at a temperature of 350°F (180°C) for about 18 minutes. Coat the bottom and two thirds up the side of a steel ring approximately 7 inches (18 cm) in diameter with the almond meringue. Fill half way with pistachio ice cream, scatter with a portion of the sour cherries drained of their syrup, and top with fiordilatte ice cream. Smooth with a spatula and allow to harden in the freezer for a few hours. In the meanwhile, grind the pistachios. In a small saucepan, bring the sugar and water to a boil. Add the pistachios and cook while stirring with a spoon until the sugar crystallizes. Pour onto a baking sheet and allow the nuts to cool. Extract the ice cream cake from the mold and garnish as desired with the remaining sour cherries, some of their syrup and the ground pistachios.

Preparation time: 1 h - Cooking time: 18' - Setting time: 2-3 h
Difficulty: high

ALPHABETICAL INDEX OF RECIPES

123

ALPHABETICAL
INDEX OF INGREDIENTS

124

All the photographs are by Academia Barilla except
©123RF, timer image; madllen/123RF, page 2;
Svetlana Foote/123RF, page 7; Thomas Perkins/123RF, page 9;
Kathleen Ellis/123RF, page 10; tobi/123RF, page 13; g215/123RF, page 14;
Svetlana Foote/123RF, pages 123 and 126; subbotina/123RF, page 125;
margouillat/123RF, page 128 and cover.

ACADEMIA BARILLA
AMBASSADOR OF ITALIAN CUISINE
IN THE WORLD

In the heart of Parma, recognized as one of the most prestigious capitals of cuisine, the Barilla Center stands in the middle of Barilla's historical headquarters, now hosting Academia Barilla's modern structure. Founded in 2004 with the aim of affirming the role of Italian culinary arts, protecting the regional gastronomic heritage, defending it from imitations and counterfeits and to valorize the great tradition of Italian cooking, Academia Barilla is where great professionalism and unique competences in the world of cuisine meet. The institution organizes cooking courses for those passionate about food culture, offering services dedicated to the operators in the sector and proposing products of unparalleled quality. Academia Barilla was awarded the "Business-Culture Prize" for its promotional activities regarding gastronomic culture and Italian creativity in the world. The headquarters were designed to meet the educational needs in the field of food preparation and have the multimedia tools necessary to host large events: around an extraordinary gastronomic auditorium, there are an internal restaurant, a multisensory laboratory and various classrooms equipped with the most modern technology. In the Gastronomic Library are conserved over 11,000 volumes regarding specific topics and an unusual collection of historical menus and printed materials on the culinary arts: the library's enormous cultural heritage is available online and allows anyone to access hundreds of digitalized historical texts. This forward thinking organization and the presence of an internationally renowned team of professors guarantee a wide rage of courses, able to satisfy the needs of both catering professionals as well as simple cuisine enthusiasts. Academia Barilla also organizes cultural events and initiatives for highlighting culinary sciences open to the public, with the participation of experts, chefs and food critics. It also promotes the "Film Award," especially for short-length films dedicated to Italian food traditions.

www.academiabarilla.it

WHITE STAR PUBLISHERS

WS White Star Publishers® is a registered trademark
property of De Agostini Libri S.p.A.

© 2015 De Agostini Libri S.p.A.
Via G. da Verrazano, 15 - 28100 Novara, Italy
www.whitestar.it - www.deagostini.it

Translation and editing: TperTradurre S.R.L.

ISBN 978-88-544-0927-9
1 2 3 4 5 6   19 18 17 16 15

Printed in China

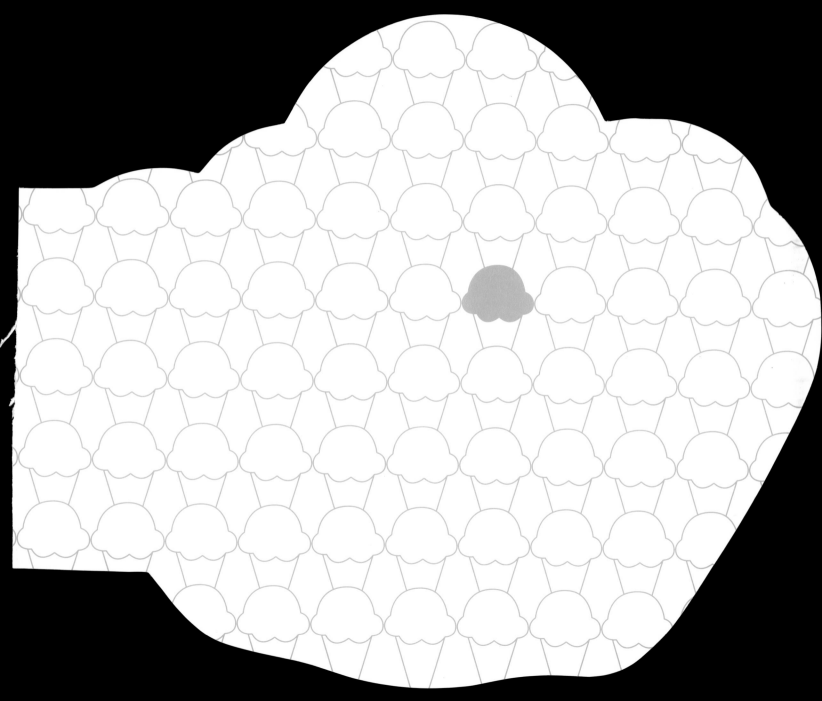

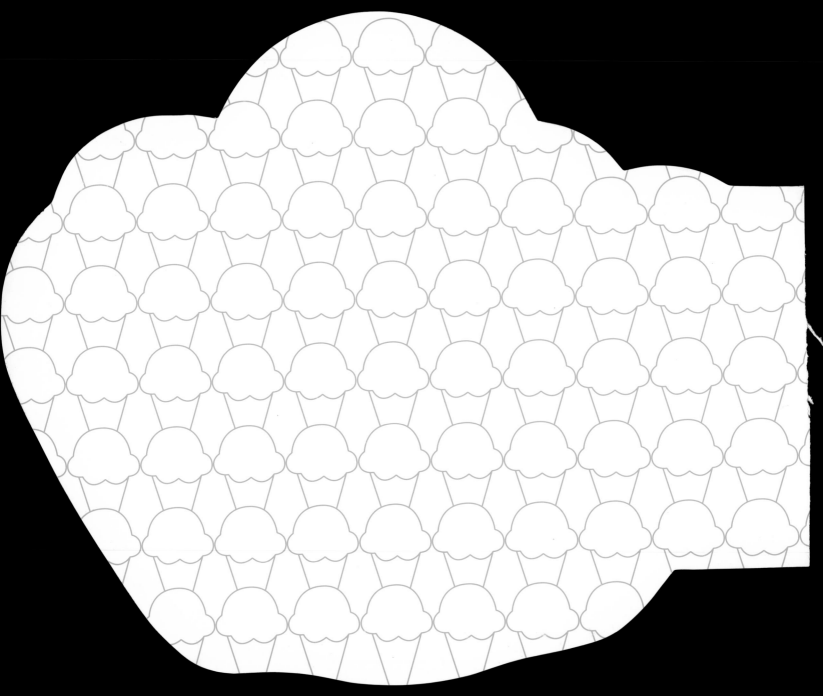